**Discovering
Cultures**

Iraq

Dana Meachen Rau

BENCHMARK BOOKS

MARSHALL CAVENDISH
NEW YORK

With thanks to Professor Ayad Al-Qazzaz, California State University, Sacramento, for the careful review of this manuscript.

Benchmark Books
Marshall Cavendish
99 White Plains Road
Tarrytown, New York 10591-9001
www.marshallcavendish.com

Library of Congress Cataloging-in-Publication Data

Rau, Dana Meachen, 1971-
Iraq / Dana Meachen Rau.
p. cm. — (Discovering cultures)
Summary: An introduction to the geography, history, people, and culture of Iraq.
Includes bibliographic references and index.
ISBN 0-7614-1726-5
1. Iraq—juvenile literature. [1. Iraq.] I. Title. II. Series.
DS70.62.R383 2004
956.7—dc22

2003019100

Photo Research by Candlepants Incorporated

Cover Photo: Corbis/Reuters NewMedia Inc.

The photographs in this book are used by permission and through the courtesy of; *Corbis*: David Turnley, 1, 20, 30, 34, 37 (lower); Caroline Penn, 4; Nik Wheeler, 8; Shepard Sherbell, 9, 14, 15, 18, 19, back cover; Thomas Hartwell, 10; Olivier Coret, 12; Francoise de Mulder, 13 (right), 38; Michael S. Yamashita, 13 (left), 22-23, 28, 33 (right), 36, 43 (top left), 43 (center); Karem Sahib, 16; AFP, 31, 37 (top); Lynsey Addario, 32, 33 (left); Antoine Serra/In Vus, 39. *Georg Gerster/Photo Researchers Inc.*: 6-7, 42 (center). *Shehzad Noorani/Peter Arnold*: 21, 26, 27, 35. *George Mattei/Envision*: 24. *Shawn Baldwin/AP Wide World Photo*: 44.

Cover: *The minaret of Samarra's mosque in Iraq*; Title page: *An Iraqi girl*

Map and illustrations by Ian Warpole
Book design by Virginia Pope

Printed in China
1 3 5 6 4 2

Turn the Pages...

Where in the World Is Iraq?

Imagine a swirling desert sandstorm, a beating hot sun, or a flash flood of a mighty river. Also imagine high mountains, fields of crops, and beautiful remains of ancient cultures. This is Iraq.

Iraq is a country on the continent of Asia. It is in an area called the Middle East. Iraq is surrounded by many other countries—Turkey in the north, Iran in the east, Kuwait and Saudi Arabia in the south, and Jordan and Syria in the west.

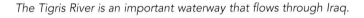

The Tigris River is an important waterway that flows through Iraq.

Map of Iraq

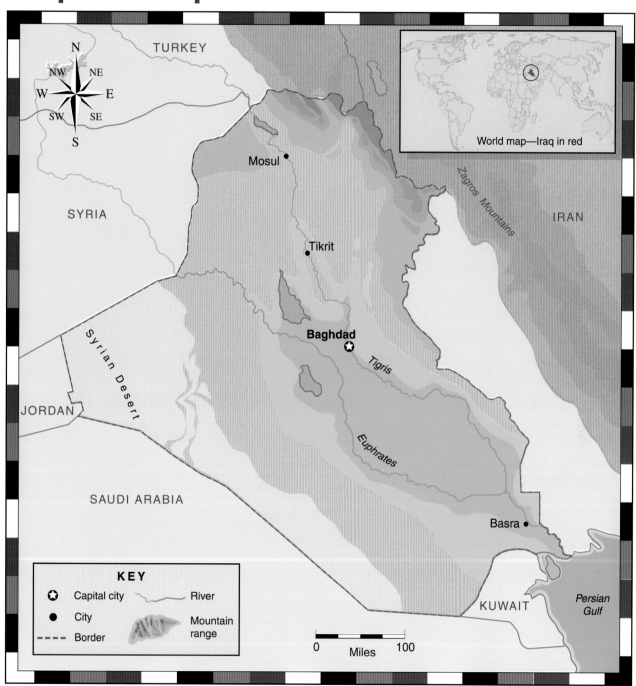

World map—Iraq in red

N
NW   NE
W   E
SW   SE
S

TURKEY

SYRIA

Mosul

Tikrit

Zagros Mountains

IRAN

Syrian Desert

Baghdad

Tigris

JORDAN

Euphrates

SAUDI ARABIA

Basra

KEY

Capital city   River

City   Mountain range

Border

0   Miles   100

KUWAIT

Persian Gulf

Only a small part of Iraq touches a large body of water. On its very southern tip, Iraq borders the Persian Gulf. This ocean leads out into the larger Arabian Sea. Two main waterways flow through the center of Iraq—the Tigris and Euphrates Rivers. These rivers have provided Iraqis with water for thousands of years.

The west and southwest of Iraq are covered in hot, sandy desert. This desert is part of the Syrian Desert. It crosses into Saudi Arabia, Jordan, and Syria. On the opposite end of Iraq, in the north and northeast, are cooler highlands. This area includes the Zagros Mountains, which Iraq shares with Iran and Turkey.

The rest of Iraq is covered with plains between the Tigris and Euphrates Rivers. The northern plain is somewhat dry. But the southern plain is rich farming land. Many Iraqis live here.

Parts of Iraq are covered with dry, sandy deserts.

Tall mountains can be found in northern Iraq.

Iraq's summer, which lasts from May to October, is very hot and dry. July and August are especially hot. Winter, which falls between December and February, is mild in most of the country. But in the higher lands of the mountains, summers are cooler and winters can be very snowy and cold.

Rain falls in the northern highlands, but it rains very little in the rest of the country. The most rain falls between October and May. When it rains, it can create floods. Dry riverbeds called *wadis* usually crisscross the deserts. But when it rains heavily, they fill up with water and become dangerous rushing rivers.

Near sources of water, Iraq is filled with lush green plants.

Most green plants, such as date palm trees, willow trees, and licorice plants, grow in southern Iraq. There is also a marshy area in the south where tall reeds and other wetland plants grow. The desert has almost no plants. Some shrubs and oak trees grow in the north.

Baghdad is Iraq's largest city and the country's capital.

Many different animals live in Iraq. Birds, such as hawks, ducks, and herons, can be seen flying through the skies. Wolves, hyenas, antelopes, and lizards live on the ground. Camels can be found in the deserts. People living here use the camels to travel across the sand.

Some of Iraq's important cities include the port of Basra and the business center of Mosul. But Baghdad, the capital of Iraq, is the country's largest city. It is located on the shores of the Tigris River. Baghdad includes an airport, highways, apartments, and business centers.

Iraq's main natural resource is oil. Drilling for oil and trading it to other countries is Iraq's most important business.

Blow, Wind, Blow!

Two types of winds often blow through Iraq. One, called the *shamal*, blows in the summer. It comes from the north and brings dry air across Iraq. The shamal keeps the summer sky free of clouds, which means the sun beats down non-stop. When the seasons change, another wind, called the *sharqi*, arrives from the south. It often carries dust and creates major blinding sandstorms.

What Makes Iraq Iraqi?

In Iraq, family is very important. Sometimes a husband and wife and their children live with the father's parents. There might even be aunts and uncles nearby. Young and old people learn from each other and pass down traditions. Iraqi people are very loyal to their families.

An Iraqi family enjoys a walk in Baghdad.

There are more than 24 million people in Iraq. About 75 percent of them are Arab, which is the ethnic group of much of the Middle East. Another ethnic group is the Kurds. They make up about 20 percent of the population. Other smaller groups are Turkomans and Assyrians. At times, these communities have not been able to live peacefully together. The Arabs and the Kurds have been fighting for many years.

One of the most important parts of Iraqi life is religion. It affects everything Iraqis do. Almost all Iraqis are Muslim and follow a religion called Islam.

Islam is based on the teachings of a holy book called the Quran. Muslims believe that a man named Muhammad who lived long ago received the Quran from Allah (God). They believe Muhammad was a *prophet* —a man sent by Allah. There are two groups of Muslims in Iraq—the Sunni

Iraqi boys in traditional Arab clothing

A Kurdish girl

13

and the Shiite. These two groups have disagreed for many years about some parts of their religion. These differences have created bitter arguments between the groups.

Muslims believe that the Quran is the word of God. Reading and studying it is very important to Iraqis. Daily prayer is also important. Muslims must pray five times a day. They pray when the sun rises, at noon, in the afternoon, when the sun sets, and in the evening. To pray, they face in the direction of the holy city of Mecca in Saudi Arabia. They bow down low, touch their foreheads to the ground, and pray quietly. Once in their lifetimes, all adult Muslims must travel to Mecca as well. But if they cannot afford the trip, they do not have to go.

On Fridays, schools and businesses are closed. Many Muslim men pray in

Mosaics cover the dome of the Al-Way Mosque, where many Muslims worship.

mosques. Here, they listen to sermons led by teachers called *imams*. The mosques are very beautiful buildings. They are often covered with *mosaics*. Muslims cannot show human or animal forms in their artwork, so the mosaics show patterns and colors instead.

Iraq's early cultures invented many things we still use today. Starting about 7,000 years ago, between the Tigris and Euphrates Rivers, the civilization of Mesopotamia grew. Many cultures lived there, including the Sumerians, the Babylonians, the Assyrians, and the Chaldeans. The Sumerians were the first to create a form of writing. They also invented the wheel and were the first to divide an hour into sixty minutes. The Babylonian king Hammurabi created the first written collection of laws. King Nebuchadnezzar II, a Chaldean king, built the Hanging Gardens of Babylon, one of the wonders of the ancient world. Today, in the many museums of Iraq where ancient treasures are kept, people are reminded of the country's rich and ancient history.

Iraqi music has a unique sound. Musicians still use many traditional instruments, such as the *oud*, which is like a small guitar. They also play the *rebaba*, a long-necked

A musician plays the oud.

Some Iraqi women wear long black cloaks called abayas.

instrument with strings played with a bow. Baghdad is the home of Iraq's National Symphony Orchestra.

Woven rugs are a traditional Iraqi art form. Mosul is known for its cloth, such as muslin, which is named for the city. Iraqis also make silver jewelry, pottery, and furniture.

In the cities, most Iraqis dress as people do in the United States. Some still wear traditional clothing, especially in the countryside. Many men wear headdresses. They may wrap a cloth around their heads like a *turban.* Or they may drape it over their heads and tie it with a black cord. This keeps their heads cool from the hot sun. Men might also wear a *caftan,* a long shirt that hangs down to the ankles.

It is a religious custom for Muslim women to keep their heads covered with a veil. Iraqi women do not have to do this, but many women and girls still do. Some women also wear an *abaya,* a black cloak that covers them from head to feet.

The Arabic Alphabet

Arabic is the official language of Iraq. There are three types of Arabic—classical, modern, and spoken. Classical Arabic is the type used in the Quran. Modern Arabic is a simpler version of classical Arabic. It is taught throughout the Arab countries. The spoken form of Arabic is used when talking, but not when writing.

The Arabic alphabet consists of twenty-eight letters. They are read and written from right to left. Beautiful images of Arabic can be seen in the pages of the Quran. It is also displayed on the walls of Iraqi mosques as part of the decoration.

أ	Alef	ر	Ra	ف	Fa
ب	Ba	ز	Zai	ق	Qaf
ت	Ta	س	Seen	ك	Kaf
ث	Tha	ش	Sheen	ل	Lam
ج	Jeem	ص	Sad	م	Meem
ح	Ha	ض	Dad	ن	Nun
خ	Kha	ط	Toa	ه	He
د	Dal	ظ	Zhoa	و	Waw
ذ	Thal	ع	Ain	ي	Ya
		غ	Ghain		

Living in Iraq

Living in Iraq today is not easy. It is a country that has been part of many wars. From 1980 to 1988, Iraq fought a war with its neighbor, Iran. In 1990, they fought with the United States after Iraq invaded Kuwait. They fought with the United States again in 2003. These wars have damaged buildings, oil fields, electric companies, *water treatment plants*, and other structures that keep the country going. The damaged water treatment plants have not been able to keep the water clean. Many people, especially children, have picked up diseases from the dirty water.

Many buildings in Iraq have been damaged by war.

A family carrying home its food rations.

The former president of Iraq, Saddam Hussein, led his country in these wars. In his desire for power, he was often cruel to people who disagreed with him. He even used weapons to hurt and kill his own people.

In 1990, the United Nations (UN), a group of representatives from countries all around the world, limited what Iraq could buy from and sell to other countries. They did this because Saddam Hussein was not following the rules of the UN. The people of Iraq suffered because they could not get the food and medicines they needed. The UN let Iraq trade oil for food and supplies. Iraqis received food *rations*, such as bread and rice, from their government.

Tall buildings fill the city skyline.

During more peaceful times, life in Iraqi cities is much like life in cities around the world. Tall office buildings, apartment buildings, and ancient monuments make up the skyline. Most Iraqis live in the cities. People drive through the streets in taxis and buses. They work in offices, factories, shops, and restaurants.

Many Iraqis live in farming villages along the Tigris and Euphrates Rivers. Their houses are made of mud bricks with thatched roofs. Farmers grow wheat, rice, barley, dates, grapes, pears, and many other crops. They also raise animals, such as cattle and sheep. Farmers must often deal with sandstorms and flooding of the rivers.

In the desert, Bedouin tribes live in a very different way. They are *nomads*, which means they move from place to place with their *clan*. A clan is a group of families, each family living in its own tents. On the desert, the Bedouin herd and raise animals, such as camels.

For more than 5,000 years, the Madan lived in the marshes in southern Iraq. They lived on small islands in houses made of reeds. The Madan traveled in boats

Traffic is heavy in Baghdad as people go to work and shop in the city.

called *mashuf*. They fished in the waters and herded water buffalo. Sadly, much of the Madan's marshland was destroyed by Saddam Hussein's troops. Because of this, the Madans were forced to leave the area.

Near the mountains in the north is the homeland of the Kurds. The Kurdish region also crosses into other neighboring countries. The culture of the Kurds is different from the rest of Iraq. In fact, they would like to have their own country. The Kurds herd and raise animals and live in houses made of stone.

All over Iraq, people enjoy a variety of foods. Meat dishes include beef, lamb, fish, or chicken. Sometimes Iraqis cook their meat as *kebabs*. Kebabs are chunks of meat and vegetables stuck onto a long stick called a skewer and then grilled. Most Iraqis do not eat pork because Islamic law forbids it. Meat is served with rice or bread. A *samoon* is a round

A Kurdish village in the north

Sweet dates are part of many Iraqi meals.

bread made from wheat. Iraqis also make stews that may include onions, garlic, tomatoes, chickpeas, and eggplants. They spice them up with chilies and curry.

Iraqis may drink coffee or tea with their meals. Arab coffee is very strong. Another drink in farming regions is milk from the water buffalo. Dessert is often fruit, as well as other sweet treats that often include dates. People also enjoy a pudding called *ma'mounia*—made with cream, butter, and cinnamon—and *baklava*, a sweet sticky pastry.

Let's Eat!
Klajah (Date Pastries)

Dates make tasty snacks and desserts. Ask an adult to help you prepare these delicious pastries.

Dough:

1 cup warm water

1 package active dry yeast

3 cups flour

1/2 teaspoon salt

1 teaspoon baking powder

1/2 tablespoon dried fennel

1 stick and 2 tablespoons unsalted butter, melted

Filling:

8 ounces pitted dates

2 tablespoons unsalted butter

1 tablespoon milk

To make the dough: Dissolve the yeast in warm water. In another bowl, combine flour, salt, baking powder, fennel, and melted butter. Add yeast and water and mix until combined. Cover the bowl with a damp towel. Let the mixture rise for about an hour, until the dough has doubled.

To make the filling: Cut up the dates into very small pieces. Put them in a double boiler with the butter and milk. Stir and cook for about 5 minutes. The mixture will become soft, like dough. When the mixture has cooled, spoon out one teaspoon and roll it into a little ball. Repeat with the rest of the mixture until you have lots of little date balls.

Putting it together: Knead the dough about ten times. Roll it out to about 1/4-inch thick with a rolling pin. Cut out 3-inch circles with a cookie cutter. Repeat until you have the same number of circles as you have balls of dates. Place a date ball in the center of a dough circle. Close the circle around the date ball and seal. Then roll it into a ball with your hands and press it flat like a cookie. Place it on a cookie sheet and repeat with the rest. Brush the tops of the pastries with a beaten egg white. Sprinkle with sesame seeds. Pierce holes in the tops with a fork. Bake at 425 degrees Fahrenheit for about 20 minutes, until lightly browned. This recipe makes about three dozen pastries.

School Days

Thousands of years ago, schools were created in southern Iraq in the ancient land of Sumeria. The only children to attend them were probably boys from very wealthy families.

Today, schooling in Iraq is very different. Education is free for all children—all the way up to college. More than half of the population can read and write. However,

Students in Iraq are eager to learn.

These boys learn metalwork at a vocational school.

more boys than girls attend school. Students value the importance of learning about their rich past, as well as learning skills they will need for the future.

Children must go to school for six years. From ages six to twelve, they attend first level, or primary school. Subjects are taught in the national language of Arabic. In the north, Kurdish children are taught in their Kurdish language.

After primary school, students may go on to junior high for three years. Then they can attend senior high for another three years. Students in senior high take classes in one of three areas—math and science, the arts and social sciences, or *vocational* subjects. Vocational classes train students for jobs in farming, business, or other fields. The classes students choose in senior high decide the types of jobs they will have when they graduate.

After senior high, students may go on to college. Iraq is known in the Middle East for its large number of scientists. Many schools teach courses in science. Baghdad has several universities, including the University of Baghdad. Universities are found also in Basra, Mosul, Tikrit, and other cities. More men than women usually attend a university.

A teacher and her students hard at work

Instead of a university, a student might go to a teaching school to learn to be a primary school teacher. Or students may attend one of the more than twenty schools around Iraq that prepare them for the working world.

For several years, the lives of Iraqi students have been disrupted by war. Their classrooms are crowded, and they do not have many supplies or tools, such as computers. Warplanes often fly overhead. It is hard to keep focused on studies when danger is nearby. At the same time, most children still play games and enjoy time with friends.

After primary school, instead of going to junior high, some children must work to help their families earn money. Young children may work as metalworkers or in other jobs in the cities. In poor rural areas, some children do not go to school at all. Schools do not even exist in some places. The children must work hard to help their families survive from day to day.

The Thousand and One Nights

Iraqis have a long tradition of storytelling. From ancient times, stories have been passed down from old to young. One of the most amazing collections of stories from ancient times still read today is *The Thousand and One Nights*, also known as *The Arabian Nights*.

In this story, King Shahriyar's wife was unfaithful to him. In order to punish all women, he married a new girl each day and then had her killed the next morning. This went on for three years, until he married the clever Sheherazade. Every night she told him a wonderful story without an ending. He would not kill her in the morning because he wanted to know the end of her stories. She told him stories for a thousand and one nights, until he finally decided not to have her killed.

Just for Fun

Men and women have very traditional roles in Iraq. The men provide for their families, while the women take care of the children and the household. However, during recent wars, women took on some less traditional roles. Men had to serve in the military for at least two years if they were older than eighteen. While the men were off fighting, women took the jobs they left behind. These women provided for their families as the men had.

A dancer teaches a ballet class.

In Iraqi culture, women and men are often separate from each other when they are not at home. At most social events, the men and boys gather in different rooms from the women and girls. During the day, while husbands are at work, women spend their time visiting friends to talk or make crafts. In their free time, men gather in coffee shops to get

Many Iraqis listen to radios to get the latest news.

the local news. In very traditional households, men shop for food. It is considered improper for women to go to the market.

Many Iraqis spend their spare time watching television, listening to the radio, or reading the newspaper. Listening to the radio is one main way Iraqis get their news. One of the favorite radio stations of teenagers is called the Voice of Iraq. It plays much the same music that teenagers listen to in the United States.

Iraqis read the Quran on a regular basis. New books are hard to afford, so some Iraqis may purchase used or photocopied ones. In Baghdad, Mutanabbi Street is filled with booths displaying what books are available to curious readers.

Soccer is by far Iraq's favorite sport. Baghdad has three stadiums that are often filled with eager fans watching the soccer teams play. Recently, Iraq started a women's soccer team, a first for many Arab countries.

Iraqis also enjoy horse racing, basketball, boxing, and volleyball. Popular board games include backgammon, dominoes, and chess. Chess players even compete in worldwide tournaments. People play sports or games on their own, or they join

A boy learns to box in a local gymnasium.

Swimming is a good way to cool off on a hot summer day.

sports clubs and play in a more organized way.

On Fridays, families have the day off. If they live near the rivers or the Persian Gulf, they may go boating. In the mountains, they might go hiking. In Baghdad, they might visit the Iraqi Museum—the largest museum in the Middle East. They might worship in the Al-Khadhimain Mosque, with its bright gold domes reaching to the sky. They might visit ancient ruins, such as the original sites of the ancient cities of Babylon and Ur.

When the hot sun finally sets, many city dwellers come outdoors to enjoy themselves. For those who cannot afford cars, bikes are a main form of transportation. People shop in the

The Al-Khadhimain Mosque in Baghdad

Men are busy playing games in a restaurant.

markets or eat at outdoor restaurants, such as those on Abu Nawas Street in Baghdad. Some people play friendly games of dominoes or backgammon on tables in the squares. They stay up late into the evening until there is a winner.

Bazaars

Bazaars are colorful, busy markets in Iraqi cities and towns. Here, people set up outdoor stalls along the street. They sell meat, spices, and fresh fruit and vegetables. Larger bazaars also sell crafts, fabrics, and furniture. In Baghdad, Rusefeh District holds a traditional bazaar. Buying and selling is not a simple process. At bazaars, customers are expected to bargain for a good price. The buyer offers less money than the item is marked. The seller may agree with the lower price, or ask for more. If they finally agree, the customer buys the item.

Let's Celebrate!

One of the holiest times of the year for Iraqis is Ramadan. Ramadan is the ninth month of the Islamic calendar. This calendar is based on the movements of the moon.

During Ramadan, the Iraqis *fast*. They do not eat or drink all day long. In cities, before the sun rises, a drum may sound to start the day of fasting. After the sun sets, a cannon fires to end the fast. The evening meal, called the *'iftar*, may start with a date, then follow with soup and a salad.

Ramadan is a time for prayer.

36

After long days of fasting, Iraqis buy treats from the market.

A young Iraqi couple

Why do Iraqis fast? It is a way to focus on prayer and think about their lives. At the end of the month of Ramadan, Iraqis celebrate Eid al-Fitr for three days. During these days, the Iraqis hold large feasts. The people of a whole village come together to eat a meal of meat, rice, and vegetables. Often wealthier families share their feast with poorer ones.

Many important celebrations in Iraq involve families. One happy celebration is a wedding. In Iraq, parents play an important role in their children's marriages. For centuries it was a tradition for parents to choose whom their children would marry. The man and woman would meet each other first to make sure they liked each other. If both

37

Children begin studying the Quran at a young age.

were happy, then the parents arranged the wedding. Today, many parents still choose whom their children will marry. But more and more people are now choosing their husbands or wives by themselves. A wedding is usually a small service including family and friends. There are parties before and after the wedding.

Another family celebration is Al-Khatma. It is not celebrated as much anymore, but may still be practiced in smaller towns. During Al-Khatma, a child reads the Quran without making any errors. Boys and girls study hard and practice for a long time. When a boy is ready, the men gather to hear him read. The women gather in a separate ceremony for a girl. Afterward, they celebrate separately as well, with parties and gifts for the boy or girl.

Muharram

Muharram is the first month of the Muslim calendar. On the tenth of this month, Muslim Shiite Iraqis celebrate the New Year. The last day of the holiday is called Ashura. On this day Iraqis remember the grandson of Muhammad, Imam Hussein, who died for his beliefs. Also on Ashura, families and villages may come together for a large meal and tell the story of Noah's Ark. Noah was a man who built an ark and filled it with a pair of every kind of animal. This saved Noah, his family, and the animals from a terrible flood that covered the Earth.

The Iraqi flag displays three stripes—red on top, white in the middle, and black at the bottom. Three green stars lie on the white stripe, and in between them is written Allahu Akbar, which means "God is great" in Arabic.

Iraqi money is called the dinar. One thousand fils equal one dinar.

Count in Arabic

English	Arabic	Say it like this:
one	wahid	WA-hid
two	itnan	ath-NAN
three	talatha	tha-LA-tah
four	arba'a	ar-ba-AH
five	khamsa	KHAM-sah
six	sitta	SIT-tah
seven	saba'a	SAH-bah
eight	tamanya	tha-MI-yah
nine	tisa	TIS-sah
ten	ashra	AH-sha-rah

Glossary

clan   A group of related families.

fast   To do without food; not eat or drink.

mosaic (moh-ZAY-ik)   A form of art that uses small tiles to create a picture.

mosque (MOSK)   A place of Islamic worship.

nomad   A person who moves from place to place.

prophet   A person who speaks for God or a god.

ration   A certain amount of food or supplies given out to people in need.

turban   A cloth that wraps around the head.

vocational   Training in a special skill in order to get a job.

water treatment plant   A place that cleans water for people to use and drink.

Fast Facts

Iraq is a country on the continent of Asia. It is in an area called the Middle East.

Two main waterways flow through the center of Iraq—the Tigris and Euphrates Rivers. These rivers have provided Iraqis with water for thousands of years.

The west and southwest of Iraq are covered in hot, sandy desert. This desert is part of the Syrian Desert. It crosses into Saudi Arabia, Jordan, and Syria.

Baghdad, the capital of Iraq, is the country's largest city. It is located on the shores of the Tigris River.

The Iraqi flag has three stripes—red on top, white in the middle, and black at the bottom. Three green stars lie on the white stripe, and in between them is written *Allahu Akbar*, which means "God is great" in Arabic.

Rain falls in Iraq's northern highlands, but it rains very little on the rest of the country. The most rain falls between October and May.

In 2003 in Iraq, 97 percent of
the people were Muslim and 3 percent
were Christian or other religions.

Iraqi money is called the
dinar. One thousand fils
equal one dinar.

Arabic is the
official language of Iraq.
There are three types of Arabic
—classical, modern,
and spoken.

Iraq's main natural
resource is oil. Drilling for
oil and trading it to other
countries is Iraq's most
important business.

As of July 2003,
there were 24,683,313 people living in Iraq.
About 75 to 80 percent of them were Arab. The Kurds
made up about 15 to 20 percent of the population.
Other smaller groups were Turkomans and
Assyrians.

Proud to Be Iraqi

Nazik Al-Malaikah (1923–   )

The daughter of two poets, Nazik Al-Malaikah started to write poetry at a very young age. She loved the Arabic language and used it to describe her world through poetry. Born in Baghdad, she studied there as well as in the United States. She wrote traditional rhyming verse and was also one of the first to introduce free verse to Arab literature. In addition, she wrote about women's issues in society. She currently lives in Egypt.

Kazem Al-Saher (1961–   )

All over the Arab world, people listen to the music of Kazem Al-Saher. He has sold more than 30 million copies of his albums to fans around the world. Al-Saher blends traditional Arabic music with modern pop music. This creates a style of music unlike any other. Born in northern Iraq, Al-Saher started playing music at a young age on the oud. He studied at the Musical Institute of Baghdad. Today he plays in worldwide tours. He performs

with an orchestra of more than thirty people. The words to Al-Saher's songs are important to him. They are like poetry. His songs speak about love for others and his love for Iraq and its people.

Jawad Salim (1920–1961)

While driving through Baghdad, one might pass the Monument of Revolution in the center of the city. The sculptor Jawad Salim created this very large modern sculpture made of bronze on marble. Salim was born in Ankara and studied art in Paris, Rome, and London. He then returned to Iraq and became an important leader of modern art. His ideas were inspired by ancient traditions and stories of the Iraqi people. He spent a large part of his life as a teacher at the Institute of Fine Arts in Baghdad.

Find Out More

Books

The Arabian Nights by Neil Philip. Orchard Books, New York, 1994.

Empires of Mesopotamia by Don Nardo. Lucent Books, San Diego, CA, 2000.

Iraq by Leila Merrell Foster. Children's Press, Danbury, CT, 1998.

Saddam Hussein by Dale Anderson. Lerner Publications Company, Minneapolis, MN, 2003.

Web Sites*

http://www.iraqsport.com

Iraq Sport details the latest sports news for fans, especially Iraq's favorite sport, soccer.

http://www.iraq4u.com/

Iraq4U.com includes the latest news from Iraq, recipes, music, and links to many Iraq Web sites, including museums, schools, and businesses.

http://www.unicef.org

The United Nations Children's Fund (UNICEF) is helping to make Iraq, and countries all over the world, safe and healthy places for children to live.

Video

Islam: Empire of Faith, PBS Home Video, VHS, 2001.

*All Internet sites were available and accurate when sent to press.

Index

Page numbers for illustrations are in **boldface.**

About the Author

Dana Meachen Rau is an author, editor, and illustrator. A graduate of Trinity College in Hartford, Connecticut, she has written almost one hundred books for children, including nonfiction, biographies, early readers, and historical fiction. Ms. Rau lives and works in Burlington, Connecticut, with her husband Chris, and children, Charlie and Allison.